SQUIRES KITCHEN'S GUIDE TO

working with
chocolate

Mark Tilling

simple techniques for impressive results

First published in September 2010 by B. Dutton
Publishing Limited, The Grange, Hones Yard,
Farnham, Surrey, GU9 8BB.
Copyright: Mark Tilling 2010
ISBN-13: 978-1-905113-18-7

Publisher: Beverley Dutton
Editor: Jenny Stewart
Art Director/Designer: Sarah Ryan
Sub Editor: Jenny Royle
Graphic Designer: Zena Manicom
Publishing Assistant: Louise Pepé
Photography: Rob Goves
Printed in China

introduction

I have been working as a pastry chef and chocolatier for over 15 years and it's been a great pleasure to work with such an amazing ingredient. I've really enjoyed bringing the skills I've learnt together and passing on my knowledge to you in this, my first book.

When I started putting the work together I wanted to present the techniques in a way that's easy to understand – throughout the book you'll find pictures of each stage and step-by-step notes to go with them. If you're a complete newcomer to chocolate, this book covers all the basics you'll need and will help you gain confidence in learning the basics. If you've worked with chocolate before, you might find it helpful to have a recap on the tempering techniques and you can pick up some handy new ideas for making different decorations.

Towards the back of the book I have given you four of my favourite yet simple recipes for making irresistible chocolate desserts, cakes, cupcakes and truffles. With each recipe you'll find some suggestions for changing the flavours a little, showing how you can make exciting and unusual chocolate creations for all occasions.

I hope you enjoy working with chocolate as much as I do.

Mark Tilling

I would like to dedicate this book to my wonderful wife Vicky – thank you for all your support over the years; you are my rock, my love, my best friend.

Thank you to Bev and Rob Dutton for letting me write this book and for your support since I have been working at Squires. Also to the staff at Squires, thank you especially to Sarah and Jenny for making this a wonderful book.

Thanks to Rob Goves for his outstanding photography.

To my parents Carole and Tony and all my family and friends.

To all at Callebaut, especially Bilkis, Simon, Debbie and Beverley.

And lastly to a very good friend of mine, Martin Nash – if not for him I would not be where I am today in my career.

Thank you all.

contents

It is important to temper chocolate before you use it to ensure that it has a good snap and shine when it is ready to eat. Many people are frightened by the idea of tempering chocolate but with a little practice you will soon get the hang of it and when you do there are endless things you can make.

There are many different ways to temper chocolate but I have chosen three different methods: in a microwave, in a bain-marie and a new way using an added ingredient, pure cocoa butter in powdered form (also known as Mycryo® and CoKrystal B).

All three methods require very little equipment so you can choose whichever suits you. It may take a few attempts to temper successfully but it is worth persevering – remember, practice makes perfect!

Before you start it is important to use a good quality chocolate, known as couverture, which contains a high percentage of cocoa butter. Avoid chocolate that has vegetable fat in it because it does not temper well and the flavour isn't as good. You can buy high quality couverture chocolate from Squires Kitchen (see suppliers on page 72) and other reputable chocolate suppliers.

tempering chocolate

tempering in a microwave

edibles

Good quality couverture chocolate
– milk, dark or white (SK)

equipment

Microwave (a domestic one is fine)
Plastic bowl suitable for use in the microwave
Plastic or metal spoon or spatula
Hairdryer or heat gun
Digital thermometer (optional – you can still
temper chocolate without one)
Palette knife

top tip

It may take you more than once to get it right as all microwaves are different – make a note of
the timings for your microwave so you can refer to them next time. Take one step at a time and
don't be tempted to rush it.

1 Place two thirds of the amount of the chocolate that you are going to temper into a bowl; the other third will be used later in the tempering process. You will need to use a microwaveable plastic bowl as porcelain will become too hot.

2 Place the bowl into the microwave and heat for 30 seconds on half power. Stir the chocolate and then return it to the microwave for another 30 seconds. Repeat this as many times as required until the chocolate has melted. Don't be tempted to rush this stage of the process as the chocolate may burn if heated for too long.

3 You will notice that the chocolate will start to melt slowly. When the chocolate has melted completely it should be around 45°C – you can test this with a digital thermometer if you have one.

4 Add the remaining third of the chocolate to the melted chocolate and stir gently (do not over-stir the chocolate). The cold chocolate will melt into the warm chocolate and will lower the temperature slightly.

5 If the cool chocolate does not melt, use a hairdryer or heat gun to melt it slowly, stirring at the same time. Take care not to overheat the chocolate. Just before all the chocolate has melted,

turn off the heat and let it finish melting by itself (this will prevent it from overheating).

6 Test the temperature of the chocolate to make sure that you have tempered it correctly. If you have a thermometer the temperatures should be as follows:
dark chocolate 31-32°C;
milk chocolate 29-30°C;
white chocolate 27-28°C.
If the chocolate is at the correct temperature it is ready to use.

7 You can also check that the chocolate is correctly tempered by dipping the end of a palette knife in the chocolate and setting it aside. If it starts to set in around 5 minutes then the chocolate is tempered and ready to use. If the chocolate does not set then it is still too hot.

8 If the chocolate is too hot, gently stir in more cool chocolate until it reaches the required temperature.

9 When you are working with the tempered chocolate it may begin to cool and thicken. Use the hairdryer or heat gun again to heat the chocolate just a little. Check the temperature as before.

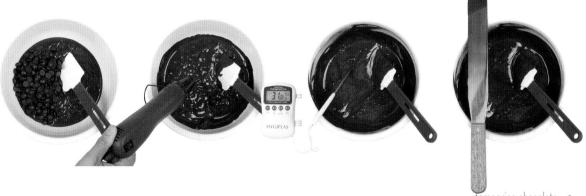

tempering in a bain-marie

edibles

Good quality couverture chocolate
– milk, dark or white (SK)

equipment

Stove top

Saucepan

Metal bowl (that does not touch the bottom of
the saucepan)

Plastic or metal spoon or spatula

Hairdryer or heat gun

Digital thermometer (optional – you can still
temper chocolate without one)

Palette knife

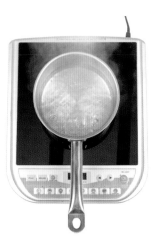

1 Pour a small amount of water into the saucepan and bring to a very gentle simmer.

2 Place the bowl on top and put two thirds of the amount of chocolate that you are using into the bowl. Stir gently with the spatula as it melts.

3 When the chocolate has melted test it with a thermometer if you have one – it should be around 45-50°C. Remove from the heat and set the bowl to one side.

4 Add the remaining third of the chocolate to the melted chocolate and stir slowly, taking care not to over-stir. This will melt into the chocolate and will also cool the chocolate slightly.

5 Use a hairdryer or heat gun to melt the chocolate, stirring at the same time. You are aiming to melt any remaining chocolate slowly – take care not to overheat the chocolate.

6 Just before all the chocolate has melted stop using the hairdryer/heat gun and let the chocolate melt in its own heat. This will also prevent it from overheating.

7 Test the temperature of the chocolate to make sure that you have tempered it correctly. If you have a thermometer the temperatures should be as follows:

    dark chocolate 31-32°C;
    milk chocolate 29-30°C;
    white chocolate 27-28°C.

The chocolate is now ready to use.

8 Another way to test the chocolate is to dip the end of the palette knife in the chocolate and set aside. If it starts to set in around 5 minutes then the chocolate is tempered and ready to use. If the chocolate does not set then it is still too hot. If this is the case, add a little more cool chocolate and stir gently. Test again before use.

9 When working with the tempered chocolate it may begin to cool and thicken. If this happens, heat a little with the hairdryer/heat gun to melt it again and test with a thermometer or palette knife, as before.

tempering with powdered cocoa butter

edibles

1kg (2lb 3¼oz) good quality couverture chocolate – dark, milk or white (SK)

10g (½oz) powdered cocoa butter (SK)

equipment

Microwave (a domestic one is fine)

Plastic bowl suitable for use in the microwave

Plastic or metal spoon or spatula

Digital thermometer

Palette knife

When tempering with powdered cocoa butter you will have a longer working time before the chocolate hardens.

Pure cocoa butter in a dry powder form can also be used for frying and as a setting agent in mousses.

1 Place the chocolate into a plastic bowl and heat in the microwave on half power for 30 seconds. Stir the chocolate and then return it to the microwave for another 30 seconds. Repeat this as many times as required until the chocolate has melted. If you have a thermometer, check that the temperature of the chocolate is 40-45°C.

2 Remove the chocolate from the microwave and allow to cool slightly. For dark chocolate, cool to 34-35°C; for milk, white or coloured chocolate cool to 33-34°C.

3 Add 10g of powdered cocoa butter to the chocolate and mix well.

4 Allow the chocolate to cool further until it is at the correct working temperature, as follows:
dark chocolate 31-32°C;
milk chocolate 29-30°C;
white chocolate 27-28°C.
The chocolate is now ready to use.

5 You can also check that the chocolate is correctly tempered by dipping the end of a palette knife in the chocolate and setting it aside. If it starts to set in approximately 5 minutes then the chocolate is tempered and ready to use. If the chocolate does not set then it is still too hot and should be left a little longer to cool.

Melted, tempered chocolate can be piped into virtually any design using the most basic of equipment – a greaseproof piping bag, a sheet of acetate and a template.

If you have piped with royal icing before you will notice that piping in chocolate is very different to work with – chocolate is much runnier so you will find that you need to be a lot quicker as you work.

You can work from any template so personalising celebration cakes, Easter eggs, wedding favours and even chocolate bars is easy once you are confident at piping with chocolate.

piping with chocolate

writing in chocolate

edibles

Bowl of tempered couverture chocolate (SK)

equipment

Piping bag
Craft knife
Small sheets of clear acetate
Lettering template

1 Prepare the lettering for your chosen inscription on a sheet of paper. Make sure this is the right size and style for the project you are working on.

2 Place a small sheet of acetate over the top of the template. Pour some melted, tempered chocolate into a piping bag and cut the tip off the bag using a craft knife.

3 To make block lettering, start by outlining the letters with the melted chocolate. Pipe directly from above to let the chocolate flow onto the acetate.

4 Leave to dry for 2 minutes before filling in the letters with more melted, tempered chocolate. Tap the acetate to level out the chocolate then let dry for 5 more minutes.

5 To pipe single-line letters, follow steps 1 and 2 then pipe onto the template following the lines with the tempered chocolate. Make sure you pipe from above to let the chocolate flow onto the acetate.

6 Allow the chocolate to set in the fridge then carefully remove from the acetate and use as required.

top tip

When piping chocolate use your index finger on the opposite hand to steady the piping bag.

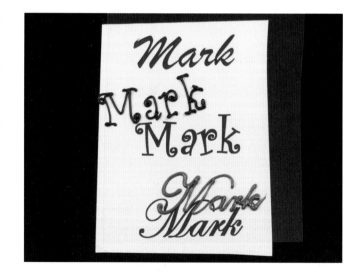

serving suggestions

Use block lettering to personalise cupcakes. When set, pipe a small amount of chocolate on the back and support in an upright position with a cocktail stick.

Personalise Easter eggs by piping the lettering onto acetate sheets, allowing to set and carefully transferring it onto a marzipan strip. To stick the lettering in position, warm the marzipan with a heat gun very, very briefly before placing it or use melted chocolate to stick it on.

Make name placements for weddings on small bars of chocolate. Trace the lettering onto the bar with a craft knife or scriber, then pipe onto this with melted chocolate.

Personalise simple 100g chocolate bars for friends and family. Pipe the lettering onto acetate sheets as described. To stick the lettering in place, warm the bar with a heat gun very, very briefly before placing the lettering or use melted chocolate to stick it on.

chocolate lattice

edibles

Bowl of tempered couverture chocolate (SK)

equipment

Piping bag
Marble slab
Craft knife
Small sheets of clear acetate

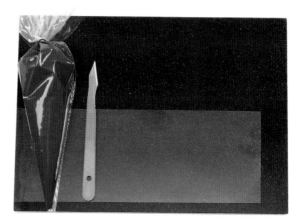

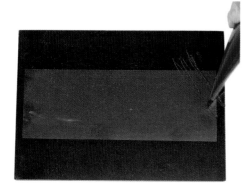

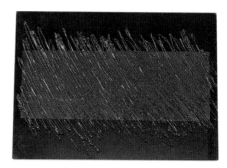

1 Fill a piping bag with melted, tempered chocolate. Cut off the end of the piping bag with the craft knife and check that the chocolate is flowing.

2 Hold the bag in one hand and pipe from one side of the acetate to the other on a slight angle. Keep piping backwards and forwards until you reach the other side of the acetate.

3 Rotate the marble slab 90° and repeat the process, piping backwards and forwards from one side to the other to create the lattice pattern.

4 Before the chocolate sets use the craft knife to find the edge of the acetate. Lift it off the marble and place to one side on a flat surface.

5 Clean off the excess chocolate from the marble slab and place the acetate (with chocolate) back on top. Allow to set.

6 Break up into small pieces or to the size required.

top tip

Make sure you cut as little as you can off the end of the piping bag before you start piping – this will make the lattice more delicate.

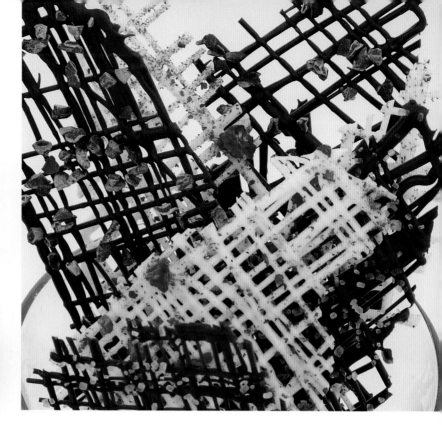

serving suggestions

Place a small piece on top of an iced chocolate cupcake.

Use white and milk chocolate to make different flavours and colours of lattice and try adding nuts, dried fruit or cocoa nibs on top before the chocolate has set. These are great to serve in a glass as an after-dinner nibble.

Place on top of a chocolate tart for an impressive finish.

Place around and on top of a glazed cake with fresh fruit.

Transfer sheets are pieces of acetate with coloured cocoa butters sprayed onto them by machine. They are simple to use and are a great way of adding a touch of colour to cakes, chocolates, cookies or desserts. There are many different designs on the market in lots of different colours to inspire your creativity.

Transfer sheets are available from cake decorating and chocolate suppliers (see page 72).

using transfer sheets

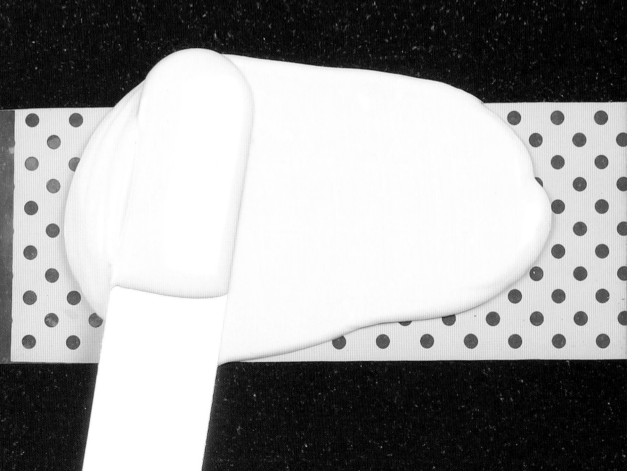

chocolate spirals

using a chocolate transfer sheet

edibles

Chocolate transfer sheet
Bowl of tempered couverture chocolate (SK)

equipment

Marble slab
Palette knife
Craft knife
Drinking straws
Ruler

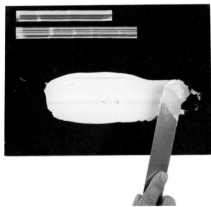

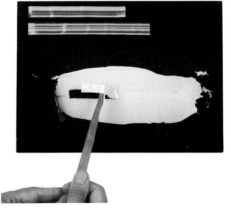

1   Using the craft knife and ruler, cut a long, thin strip of the transfer sheet to the size that you require.

2   Place the strip onto the slab, making sure the rough (not shiny) side is facing upwards.

3   Using the palette knife, spread some tempered chocolate over the strip to about 3mm thick.

4   Before the chocolate sets, use the craft knife to lift the strip off the slab and tip the excess chocolate back into the bowl.

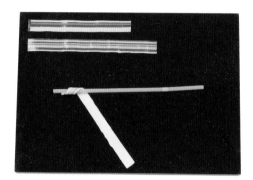

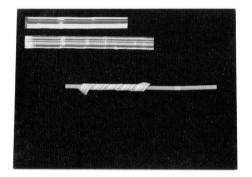

5 Place the strip back onto the slab at an angle. Place a straw horizontally on top of the strip at one end.

6 Roll the straw along the strip so that the chocolate spirals around the straw.

7 Place in the fridge for about 10 minutes until the chocolate has set.

8 Remove the straw and then carefully peel off the strip of acetate: the pattern will be transferred to the chocolate.

top tip

Start by making shorter spirals as they are easier to handle. When you are more confident, make longer ones by rolling the transfer sheet around a larger cylinder such as a rolling pin or piece of food-grade plastic piping.

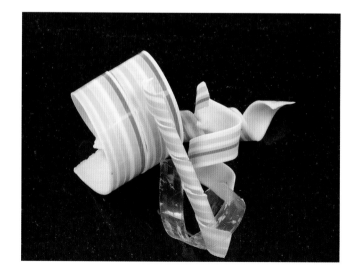

serving suggestions

Make 10 to 15 spirals and place them in the centre of a birthday or celebration cake.

Place 2 or 3 mini spirals on top of a cupcake baked in a co-ordinating cupcake case.

Place mini spirals on top of mini cakes – these are ideal for a wedding cake display or for a special afternoon tea.

To finish off a dessert, make larger spirals to wrap around mousses or iced parfaits and garnish with mini spirals.

chocolate transfer tiles

edibles

Chocolate transfer sheet
Bowl of tempered couverture chocolate (SK)

equipment

Ruler
Palette knife
Craft knife
Greaseproof paper
Small baking tray

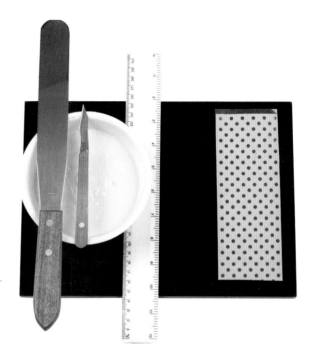

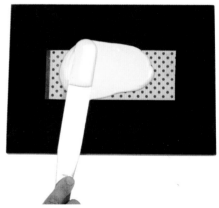

1 Cut the transfer sheet into long rectangles measuring about 30cm x 10cm. Make sure the height (short side) is around 1cm taller than the height of the cake. Lay the sheet rough side up on a work surface.

2 Pour some tempered chocolate onto the sheet and use the palette knife to spread the chocolate evenly over the transfer sheet and over the edges. The thinner the chocolate the more delicate the tiles will be.

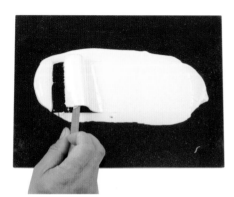

3 Use the craft knife to lift the transfer sheet carefully off the work surface and place to one side. Clean the work surface before replacing the transfer sheet back in position. (This must be done quickly before the chocolate sets.)

4 When you see the surface of the chocolate change from shiny and wet to matt and semi-firm but still pliable you can cut it into shapes.

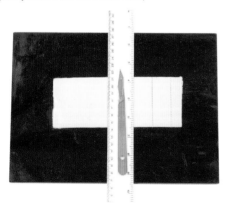

5 Use the width of the ruler as a size guide and cut the tiles with a craft knife. Make sure you only cut through the chocolate, not the acetate sheet.

6 Lay a sheet of greaseproof paper on top of the chocolate then place a small baking tray on top. This will ensure that the chocolate does not curl up when drying.

7 Leave on the surface to dry for about 20 minutes or, if the chocolate is on a work board, place in the fridge for 10 minutes.

8 Carefully upturn the transfer sheet when the chocolate has set and peel away the acetate.

If the transfer pattern does not come away from the acetate, leave the chocolate to set for a little longer. Do not be tempted to rush it.

serving suggestions

Place a chocolate tile upright on top of an iced cupcake. For weddings with a colour scheme, match the colour and pattern of the transfer with the cupcake cases.

Spread the sides of a celebration cake with ganache then stick the tiles in position so that they overlap.

Layer the tiles with fruit mousse to create a fruit and chocolate millefeuille tower.

Use the tiles to garnish desserts for a quick and impressive finish.

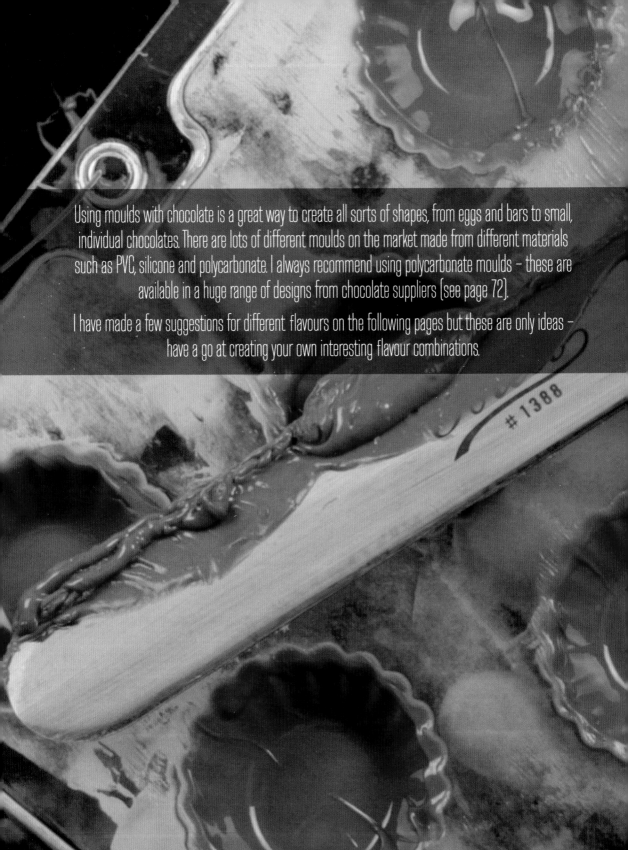

Using moulds with chocolate is a great way to create all sorts of shapes, from eggs and bars to small, individual chocolates. There are lots of different moulds on the market made from different materials such as PVC, silicone and polycarbonate. I always recommend using polycarbonate moulds – these are available in a huge range of designs from chocolate suppliers (see page 72).

I have made a few suggestions for different flavours on the following pages but these are only ideas – have a go at creating your own interesting flavour combinations.

using moulds

making a chocolate bar

edibles

Bowl of tempered couverture chocolate (SK)
Mixture of nuts or dried fruit (optional)

equipment

Chocolate bar mould
Piping bag
Craft knife

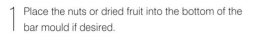

1 Place the nuts or dried fruit into the bottom of the bar mould if desired.

2 Place some melted, tempered chocolate into a piping bag and cut off the end. Start to pipe the chocolate into the mould. Pipe just to the top – make sure that you don't overfill the mould.

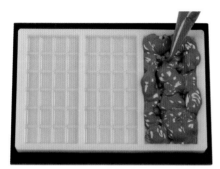

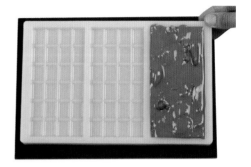

3 Tap the mould on its edge to level out the chocolate. Leave to cool at room temperature until the surface of the chocolate has changed from shiny to matt.

4 Place in the fridge for about 20 minutes until set then turn out the chocolate bar from the mould. If the bar does not come out cleanly from the mould, place back in the fridge for a few more minutes before trying again.

top tip

Buy polycarbonate moulds if you can – they will last much longer than PVC or silicone moulds.

serving suggestions

Pipe two different tempered chocolates into the mould to make a double chocolate bar.

Use freeze-dried fruits such as strawberries or raspberries to give a fruity flavour.

Try placing pistachios into the bottom of the mould to give a sweet and nutty flavour.

Add roasted cocoa nibs to the bar to give a stronger cocoa flavour and a crunchy texture.

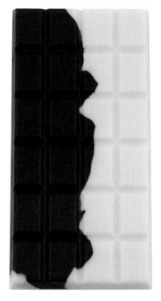

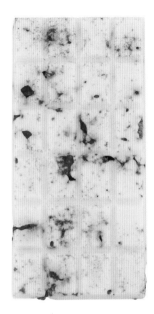

chocolate cups

edibles

Bowl of tempered couverture chocolate (SK)

equipment

Piping bag
Craft knife
Chocolate cup mould
Silicone paper (optional)
Large palette knife

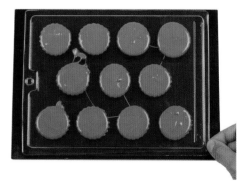

1 Pour some melted, tempered chocolate into a piping bag and cut the tip off the bag with a craft knife.

2 Pipe the chocolate into the cavities of the mould, filling each one to the top.

3 Use your hand to vibrate the mould on a work surface to remove any air bubbles in the chocolate.

4 Turn the mould upside down over a sheet of silicone paper or a clean work surface so the chocolate floods out.

5 Give the mould a little tap when it is upside down to remove any excess chocolate – this will make the cups nice and thin.

6 Use a large palette knife to scrape the excess chocolate off the mould whilst holding it upside down. Turn the mould over and scrape again.

7 Leave the chocolate to set at room temperature for about 10 minutes until the surface has gone from shiny to matt. At this stage, place into the fridge for 20 minutes.

8 Remove from fridge and release the chocolate cups from the mould.

top tip

If the chocolate does not come out of the mould easily, place it back into the fridge for a few more minutes.

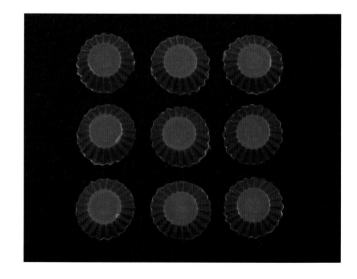

serving suggestions

Fill the base of the chocolate cup with a small amount of strawberry jam, pipe strawberry buttercream on top of this and garnish with pink sugar hearts. These are perfect for a girl's birthday party or afternoon tea.

Fill each cup with a simple chocolate ganache that has been whipped up to make it light and fluffy and piped with a star nozzle. Finish with a chocolate fan and present on a cake plate or acrylic stand.

For an after-dinner treat, soak a small disc of sponge that will fit in the bottom of the cup in espresso coffee. Place into the cup, pipe creamy buttercream on top and decorate with mini silver chocolate hearts.

For irresistible sweet canapés fill with chocolate mousse and finish with a chocolate gold bar and cocoa nibs.

By using a small marble or granite slab you can create a whole host of chocolate decorations. You can discover quick and effective ways of decorating all sorts of cakes and desserts, adding a delicate touch and using very little equipment.

It is essential that the slab is frozen in order for the chocolate to set quickly, so make sure you buy one that fits in your freezer. They are inexpensive to buy – chocolate suppliers will have them, or look out for chopping boards or even placemats made from marble or granite in kitchen shops and supermarkets.

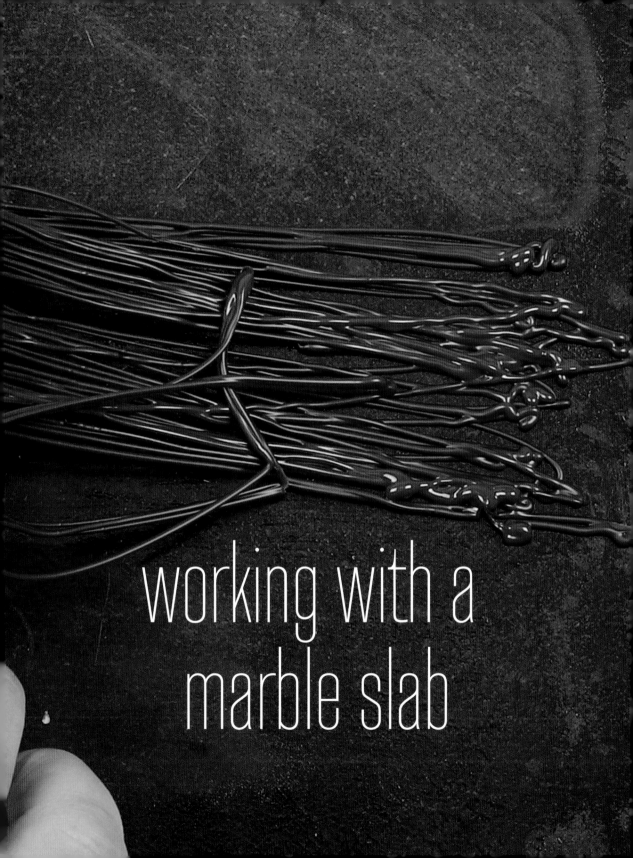

working with a
marble slab

chocolate fans

edibles

Bowl of tempered couverture chocolate (SK)

equipment

Small marble or granite slab, frozen
Craft knife
Palette knife
Kitchen towel

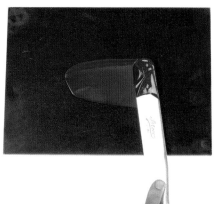

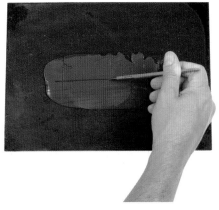

1 Place the marble slab in the freezer for a minimum of 3 hours (overnight if possible).

2 Use the end of a palette knife to pick up a small amount of melted, tempered chocolate.

3 Spread the chocolate onto the frozen slab – aim to make a rough rectangle shape.

4 Very quickly use the craft knife to cut down the chocolate lengthways and to cut off the two ends. You should end up with two long rectangular strips, each with a rough edge along one of the longest sides.

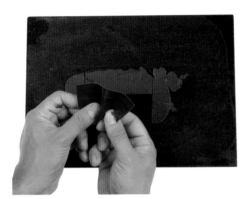

5 Using the fingertips on both hands, pick up one of the strips. Hold it with the rough edge towards you and the cut edge facing away from you.

6 Start to concertina the rough edge, making sure you pinch all the ends together to create a fan shape.

7 Repeat with the second strip. Set the 2 fans aside. Wipe the slab clean with some kitchen towel and start again.

8 The slab will start to warm up so you will only get time to make about 20 fans at a time. When this happens place the slab back in the freezer for about 20 minutes. Once it is frozen you can continue to make more fans.

top tip

This is a great decoration as it is very quick to make and is an easy way to cover a cake. If you are covering a large cake or decorating a wedding cake you may need to have two marble slabs that you can alternate so you are always working on a cold surface.

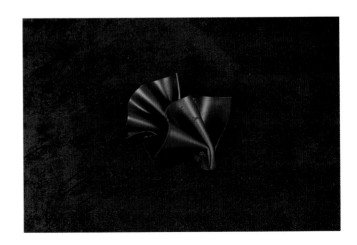

top tip

Try using 2 different types
of coloured chocolates and
marbling them together before
spreading onto the frozen slab.

serving suggestions

Cover a large celebration cake
with fans, starting at the top and
working your way down the cake.
Use melted chocolate to hold them
in place and add a few chocolate
roses and leaves between them.

Decorate cupcakes by arranging
two or three fans on the top.

To top off a dessert use white
chocolate to make the fans.
Use dessert glasses to give a
professional look.

Place 3 or 4 fans on top of mini
cakes to decorate. These make
great individual wedding cakes.

chocolate nests

edibles

Bowl of tempered couverture chocolate (SK)

equipment

Small marble or granite slab, frozen
Small piping bags
Sharp knife
Scissors

1 Place a marble slab in the freezer for a minimum of 3 hours, preferably overnight. Take it out of the freezer when you are ready to pipe, making sure it is frozen.

2 Fill a piping bag with tempered chocolate and cut off the very tip with scissors. Make the hole to the

size you require for the project – for chocolate nests, the smaller the hole, the better.

3 Working very quickly start piping from one side of the slab to the other – it doesn't matter if the lines cross over but make sure they still go side to side.

4 As soon as you have enough piped lines, quickly
use the sharp knife to lift the chocolate off the
marble.

5 Using the very tips of your fingers so as not to
melt the chocolate, mould the piped chocolate
into a nest or wrap it around a cake.

top tip

If you are making lots of nests,
place 2 or more marble slabs
in the freezer so you are always
working on a frozen surface.

serving suggestions

Make small, ball-shaped nests as a contemporary garnish for desserts and ice cream.

At Easter, make a small nest and fill with eggs or make mini nests to place on top of cupcakes.

Make a large nest, fill with ice cream or sorbet and garnish with berries.

Wrap the nest around a cake and garnish with fresh, non-toxic flowers to give an unusual finish to a birthday cake.

Once you are familiar with a basic recipe, making simple alterations is a great way of creating new and interesting dishes with minimum effort. The following four basic recipes show you how you can change them and decorate them for all sorts of celebrations such as weddings and birthdays, right down to a dinner party at home or teatime with the family.

I have finished off each idea using the some of the decorations shown in the first part of the book and some ready-made decorations from Squires Kitchen (see stockists on page 72).

recipes

chocolate truffles

edibles

500g (1lb 1½oz) dark couverture chocolate, 70-80% cocoa solids (SK)

250ml (8¾fl oz) whipping cream

40g (1½oz) butter

1 vanilla pod

300g (10½oz) tempered dark couverture chocolate for coating (SK)

100g (3½oz) cocoa powder

equipment

Stove top

Saucepan

Sharp knife

Digital thermometer (optional)

Large bowl

Spoon or spatula

Airtight container

Melon scoop or teaspoon

Food-grade plastic disposable gloves

1 Pour the cream into a saucepan. Cut down the length of the vanilla pod and place the seeds and pod into the cream. Heat the cream and vanilla in a saucepan.

2 Just before the cream boils, remove from the heat and leave to cool to around 70°C.

3 Place the chocolate in a large bowl. Remove the pod from the cream and pour over the chocolate.

4 Stir very slowly to melt the chocolate and make a smooth emulsion.

5 Pour into an airtight container and leave to set overnight in the fridge.

6 Use a melon scoop or a spoon to make small truffle balls from the chocolate and cream mixture, then set aside to harden.

7 Using gloves or a spoon roll or dip the centres into the melted tempered chocolate then into the cocoa powder. When set, roll again to knock off the excess cocoa powder.

 top tip Using a melon spoon will make your truffles more rounded than using a teaspoon. If you would like to make perfect spheres, pipe the cream and chocolate mix into truffle shells before chilling in the fridge.

mint infusion

extras

30g (1¼oz) fresh mint leaves

Icing sugar

1. When the cream has boiled add 200g of fresh mint and infuse for 20 minutes before straining and adding to the chocolate.

2. Follow the basic method to make the truffle centres then roll in icing sugar instead of cocoa powder.

very berry

extras

125ml (4½fl oz) mixed berry purée

Icing sugar

Rose Professional Dust Food Colour (SK)

(You will only need 125ml (4½fl oz) of whipping cream)

1. Reduce the cream by half and add 125ml of mixed berry purée.

2. Follow the basic method then roll in icing sugar mixed with pink dust colour instead of cocoa.

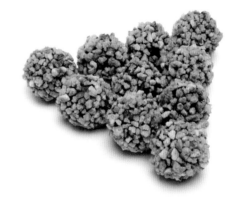

golden nugget

extras

20g (¾oz) freshly grated ginger

Classic Gold Professional Metallic Lustre Dust Food Colour (SK)

1 Add 20g of freshly grated ginger to the cream before heating then make the centres in the same way as for the standard recipe.

2 Roll in a mixture of cocoa powder and gold food dust.

nuts about truffles

extras

75g (2½oz) Nutella

Roasted nibbed hazelnuts

1 Add 75g of Nutella to the cream after it has boiled and follow the basic method.

2 Roll the centres in melted dark chocolate then in roasted nibbed hazelnuts.

chocolate cupcakes
with chocolate butter frosting

edibles

cupcakes

125g (4½oz) unsalted butter

125g (4½oz) caster sugar

2 medium eggs

50g (1¾oz) cocoa powder, sieved

75g (2½oz) self-raising flour, sieved

35ml (2tbsp) milk

frosting

200g (7oz) icing sugar

100g (3½oz) cocoa powder

250g (8¾oz) butter

75ml (4tbsp) water

equipment

Electric mixer

Large metal spoon

12-hole baking pan

Cupcake cases

Piping bag

Star nozzle

makes 12 cupcakes

1 Preheat the oven to 160°C (320°F/gas mark 3). Cream the butter and sugar together.

2 Add the eggs one at a time and beat until smooth and fluffy. Using a large spoon fold in the sieved flour and cocoa powder.

3 Place the cupcake cases into a 12-hole baking pan and spoon in the mix to two-thirds fill the cases.

4 Bake in the oven for 10-12 minutes or until cooked. Remove from the oven and leave to cool on a wire rack.

5 Make the topping by placing the icing sugar, cocoa powder, butter and water in a mixer with a whisk attachment. Mix until lighter in colour and fluffy.

6 When the cupcakes are cool, place the frosting into a piping bag with a star nozzle and pipe the icing onto the cupcakes. Make sure the cakes are completely cool before you start piping.

top tip

Always make sure that the butter and eggs are at room temperature: if you take them out of the fridge about 30 minutes before you start they will mix better.

chocolate mojito cupcakes

[this one is for the adults]

extras

2 limes

70ml (2½fl oz) white rum

50g (1¾oz) sugar

50ml (1¾fl oz) water

Fresh mint

Chocolate fan (see page 46) with mint oil

1 Make the cupcake recipe as normal but add the zest and juice of a lime when you mix in the flour.

2 To make the sugar syrup, place the sugar and water into a pan and boil for 3 minutes. After the cupcakes are baked and while they are still slightly warm, mix 50ml of white rum and the sugar syrup together and brush a little on top of each cupcake so that it soaks in.

3 Make the chocolate topping as normal and add the zest and juice of a lime and 20ml of white rum.

4 Finish with a sprig of fresh mint and make a mint chocolate fan by adding a drop of mint oil to the tempered chocolate.

rocky road chocolate cupcakes

extras

100g (3½oz) chocolate chip cookies

30g (1¼oz) dark couverture chocolate (SK)

30g (1¼oz) white chocolate (SK)

20g (¾oz) Milk Chocolate Shavings (SK)

30g (1¼oz) mini marshmallows

Chocolate transfer spirals (see page 26)

1 Make the cupcakes as normal but add 50g of broken cookies and 30g of dark and white chocolate chopped up into small pieces when you add the flour.

2 Bake and ice the cupcakes following the original recipe.

3 Decorate with more broken cookies, chocolate shavings, mini marshmallows and chocolate spirals.

chocolate easter cupcakes

spicy chocolate cupcakes

extras

60g (2¼oz) dark couverture chocolate (SK)

Small chocolate nest (see page 50)

Mini chocolate eggs

Antique Gold Professional Metallic Lustre Dust (SK)

extras

5ml (1tsp) mixed spice

5ml (1tsp) ground ginger

5ml (1tsp) ground cinnamon

200g (7¼oz) mixed candied fruit

100g (3½oz) Chocolate Mini Canes (SK)

1 Chop the dark chocolate into small pieces and add to the cupcake mix at the same time as the flour.

2 Bake and ice as normal then decorate with a small chocolate nest.

3 Use a little tempered chocolate to stick on the mini chocolate eggs. Brush a little edible gold dust on the nest and eggs.

1 Make the cupcakes as normal but add the mixed spice, cinnamon and ginger to the mix when you add the flour.

2 Make the topping as before but add the other spices before piping it on top of the cupcakes.

3 Decorate with candied fruit and chocolate mini canes.

chocolate celebration cake

edibles

65g (2¼oz) butter

75g (2½oz) dark couverture chocolate (SK)

125ml (4½fl oz) golden syrup

175g (6¼oz) self-raising flour

65g (2¼oz) light brown sugar

25g (1oz) cocoa powder

3ml (½tsp) baking powder

1 egg

equipment

20.5cm (8") round cake tin, lined with greaseproof paper

Large bowl

Electric mixer

Spatula

1 Preheat the oven to 180°C (350°F/gas mark 4). Place the butter, chocolate and golden syrup into a large bowl and add 250ml of boiling water. Mix until combined.

2 Place the flour, cocoa powder, sugar and baking powder in an electric mixer with the paddle attachment.

3 Add the egg and start mixing on a slow speed. Slowly add the chocolate mixture and mix until it becomes a smooth paste.

4 Place the mixture into a lined cake tin and bake for 45-50 minutes or until a skewer inserted in the centre comes out clean. When baked, remove from the oven and allow to cool completely.

top tip Try using silicone cake moulds instead of tins – they produce good results and are very easy to clean.

black forest indulgence cake

extras

100g (3½oz) chopped, semi-dried cherries

500ml (17½fl oz) Chantilly cream

200g (7¼oz) freshly poached cherries

1 Add some chopped, semi-dried cherries to the sponge at the end of mixing when folding in the flour.

2 When the cake is baked, fill with Chantilly cream and freshly poached cherries.

chocolate and lime wedding cake

extras

2 limes

Chocolate ganache (SK)

Pink dotty chocolate transfer tiles (see page 30)

White chocolate shavings (SK)

Pink sugar sprinkles

Extra tiers: 15cm (6") halve the recipe

25.5cm (10") double the recipe

1 To make a zesty base for a wedding cake add the zest and juice of 2 limes to the melted chocolate mixture.

2 Fill and cover the cake with a lime ganache as well to it give an even more zesty taste – you can make your own or add lime zest and juice to ready-made ganache.

double chocolate easter cake

extras

150g (5¼oz) chocolate chips
Cocoa liquor (SK Cocopave)*
Cocoform (SK)
Sugarpaste
Fresh flowers (non-toxic)
Chocolate nests (see page 50)

1 Add chocolate chips at the end of mixing and replace the chocolate in the recipe for cocoa liquor to get a more intense chocolate flavour.

2 Coat the cake with an equal mixture of Cocoform modelling chocolate and sugarpaste. Garnish with chocolate nests and fresh flowers to make a teatime treat for Easter.

*Cocoa liquor is a chocolate product made from finely ground cocoa beans. It is also known as unsweetened baking chocolate and Cocopave.

Spicy loaf cake

extras

5 cardamom pods
Chocolate fans (see page 46)
Chocolate buttercream
Fresh raspberries

1 I love mixing spices with chocolate. To make a spicy cake, place 5 crushed cardamom pods into the boiling water and allow to infuse for around 10 minutes.

2 After this time, re-boil the water then remove the seeds and add the water to the chocolate mixture as above.

3 Bake the cake in a loaf tin and decorate with chocolate buttercream, fans and raspberries for a great afternoon tea.

chocolate mousse

edibles

75ml (2½fl oz) water

50g (1¾oz) glucose

1 leaf gelatine

250g (8¾oz) dark couverture chocolate (SK)

500ml (17½fl oz) double cream

equipment

Plastic bowl suitable for use in the microwave

Microwave or bain-marie (see page 10)

Saucepan

Stove top

Measuring jug

Mixer with whisk

Spatula

serves 8-10

1 Warm the chocolate in a microwave or over a bain-marie. Heat the chocolate gently so that it doesn't burn. When melted, set the chocolate to one side.

2 Soak the gelatine in water for 5 minutes or until the gelatine leaf is soft.

3 Measure 75ml of water into a saucepan, add the glucose and bring almost to the boil.

4 Remove from the heat and leave to cool slightly before adding the soaked gelatine. Stir until all the gelatine is melted.

5 Add the water/gelatine mixture to the melted chocolate to make a thick sauce.

6 Semi-whip the cream and fold into the chocolate. Place into bowls or glasses and serve.

top tip

Use a chocolate that is high in cocoa solids – I would use a chocolate that contains around 80% cocoa solids.

Make sure you use a microwave-safe, plastic bowl in the microwave – glass and Pyrex bowls hold the heat and are more likely to cause the chocolate to burn.

chocolate cocktail

extras

50ml (1¾fl oz) rum
Piping bag with star nozzle
Caramelised cocoa nibs*
Raspberries
Caramel sauce

1 Replace 50ml of the water in the recipe with 50ml of rum to make alcoholic chocolate mousse.

2 Pipe into cocktail glasses with caramel sauce and finish with caramelised cocoa nibs and raspberries. Makes about 10 glasses.

*To caramelise the cocoa nibs, heat 40g (1½oz) of caster sugar in a pan, stirring continuously with a wooden spoon. When the sugar caramelises, add 20g (¾oz) of cocoa nibs, stir until coated then leave to cool on a tray lined with greaseproof paper. Chop into small pieces.

spicy chocolate mousse

extras

5ml (1tsp) mixed spice
Chocolate transfer cups
Chocolate truffles (see page 56)
Chocolate fans (see page 46)

1 Add 1 teaspoon of mixed spice to the water and follow the recipe as described.

2 Pipe into chocolate cups made from a coloured transfer sheet and finish with a chocolate truffle and chocolate fans. Makes about 8.

orange and chocolate mousse

extras

2 oranges

Small dessert rings

Thin discs of sponge (made from a Victoria sponge mix)

Fresh berries

Chocolate transfer spirals (see page 26), candy cane design

1 To make an orange chocolate mousse add the zest and juice of 2 oranges to the water in the recipe and finish the mousse the same way.

2 Spoon into small dessert rings with a small disc of sponge on the bottom and garnish with fresh berries and spirals of candy cane transfer sheets. Makes about 8.

raspberry and chocolate mousse cake

extras

Double the ingredients in basic recipe

200g (7¼oz) fresh raspberries

200g (7¼oz) digestive biscuits, crushed

30g (1¼oz) butter, melted

25.5cm (10") round, loose-bottomed tin

Greaseproof paper

Chocolate fans (see page 46)

1 Double the ingredients for the recipe and follow the same method. At the end when folding in the cream add 200g of fresh raspberries.

2 Line the base of the cake tin with greaseproof paper. Mix the crushed biscuits and melted butter together and push firmly into the base of the tin. Spoon the mousse mixture on top and allow to set in the fridge.

3 Carefully remove the mousse from the tin and place onto a flat dish. Use lots of chocolate fans to make an eye-catching celebration cake.

suppliers

Squires Kitchen, UK
3 Waverley Lane
Farnham
Surrey
GU9 8BB
0845 61 71 810
+44 1252 260 260
www.squires-shop.com

Squires Kitchen International School
The Grange
Hones Yard
Farnham
Surrey
GU9 8BB
0845 71 71 812
+44 1252 260 262
www.squires-school.co.uk

Squires Kitchen, France
www.squires-shop.fr

Squires Kitchen, Spain
www.squires-shop.es

SK stockists

Jane Asher Party Cakes
London
020 7584 6177

Blue Ribbons
Surrey
020 8941 1591

Catering Complements
Kent
01892 513745

Lawsons Ltd.
Devon
01752 892543

The Sugarcraft Emporium
Worcestershire
01527 576703

Surbiton Art & Sugarcraft
Surrey
020 8391 4664

SK distributors

Guy Paul & Co. Ltd.
Buckinghamshire
www.guypaul.co.uk

Culpitt Ltd.
Northumberland
NE63 8UQ
www.culpitt.com

manufacturers

Callebaut
www.callebaut.com

Cacao Barry
www.cacao-barry.com